The Complete Tool Kit For Personal and Professional Success

The Complete Tool Kit For Personal and Professional Success

The Workbook

CAROLYN ROBINSON

Copyright © 2017 **Carolyn Robinson**
All rights reserved.

ISBN-13: 9781540791832
ISBN-10: 1540791831

Contents

Introduction ·vii

One	Evaluating What You Believe · 1
Two	Is Toxic Shame Holding You Back? · · · · · · · · · · · · · · · · · 6
Three	Developing Healthy Self-Esteem · · · · · · · · · · · · · · · · · · ·14
Four	Understanding Codependency · 20
Five	Managing Your Anger · 28
Six	Taking Accountability ·38
Seven	Pulling It All Together · 44
Eight	Walking in Victory ·51

Bibliography ·53

Introduction

This workbook is designed to give you the tools you will need to identify the self-defeating beliefs that are holding you back personally and professionally. You will be taught strategies that you can use to overcome those obstacles. As you participate in this program, you will begin to see that everything you do is based on your belief system. Utilizing this newfound insight will help you reach your life goals and live a more fulfilled and meaningful life. Since your beliefs affect so many areas of your personality, we are going to use a multistep process to change your life. Over the course of our time together, we are going to explore several core areas of your personality.

In order to help you achieve the greatest level of success, we are going to ask you to take some healthy risks and develop a support group to continue moving forward in your recovery journey. Your support group will be able to offer you continued encouragement and hold you accountable for any old behaviors and habits that need to be eliminated or modified. Remember, this is a process, so be kind to yourself throughout your journey.

One

Evaluating What You Believe

*H*ave you ever wondered why some people succeed at everything they do while others never get ahead? This is an age-old question, and the answer remains the same. Our beliefs control our behaviors and attitudes and determine our comfort zones (including the people we choose to associate with).

Most people believe that we make our decisions based upon our known knowledge, using the conscious mind. This simply isn't true. Decisions are actually made by the subconscious mind, better known as the heart. There is an old proverb that says, "As a man thinks in his heart, so is he." Whether you think you can or you think you can't, you are right.

Listed below is a chart based on Bruce Threewitt's PowerPoint presentation entitled "Rebuilding Your Career". Bruce was a presenter who collaborated with the Accent Program helping individuals get jobs once they were released from jail or prison. In his power point, it indicates which tasks are carried out by the conscious mind and which are carried out by the subconscious mind.

Conscious Mind	**Subconscious Mind (Heart)**
• logic and reasoning	• single-task completion
• short-term memory	• emotions
• will	• long-term memory
• attention or focus	• beliefs
• sensory processing	• habits, attitudes, reflexes
• conscience	• self-image
• single-task completion	• multitasking

Every decision you make comes from a belief located in the subconscious mind. Holding on to beliefs that are harmful to you severely limits your ability to achieve your full potential. In order to overcome the hurts from your past, you must be intentional about your thoughts and rewrite the distorted beliefs that prevent you from achieving greatness.

In the space provided below, list some distorted beliefs that you are now aware of. If you are unaware of your distorted beliefs, begin to pay attention to your internal dialogue. For example, you may say things to yourself like, "I am stupid," "I can't do it," "I will never be able to trust anyone again," and so on.

1.
2.
3.
4.
5.

For each item listed, indicate how the belief is holding you back. For example, you may be unwilling to take healthy risks, fearful of trusting others, afraid of rejection, and so on.

1.
2.
3.

The Complete Tool Kit For Personal and Professional Success

4.
5.

If you are going to step into your destiny and fulfill your goals in life, you have to begin to identify and change those self-defeating beliefs. Otherwise you will be destined to keep repeating your dysfunctional thoughts, behaviors, and actions.

Now that you have identified your distorted beliefs, you can begin to change them.

For each distorted belief listed above, record a healthy belief to replace it. For example, if your old belief is "I am stupid," your new belief should be "I am intelligent." Once you create your list, repeat your positive statements daily.

1.
2.
3.
4.
5.

We want you to begin to use these new beliefs to rewrite your negative self-messages. Look in the mirror and state your new affirmations to yourself daily. At the beginning of this process, you may feel as if you're lying to yourself. This is a normal response. Remember, you didn't create your distorted beliefs overnight, so it is going to take some time to change your old way of thinking and feeling. It may take you several weeks to feel comfortable saying your affirmations every day. Work through your discomfort. If you stick to this, we guarantee that your outcome will be far greater than any amount of embarrassment you may have felt initially.

In addition to the beliefs listed above, we also recommend that you use religious scriptures, poems, songs, or inspirational quotes to affirm yourself. You can list any additional affirmations in the space provided below.

1.
2.

3.
4.
5.

How Is Our Belief System Formed?

According to Keith Johnson, author of *The Confidence Makeover*, two-thirds of our beliefs are formed between birth and age seven. Child-development professionals refer to this stage as the formative years. During this time, children are heavily influenced by their parents or caregivers. Consequently, if you were raised in an abusive or dysfunctional family, there is a strong chance that you may have developed unhealthy beliefs about yourself, others, and the world you live in.

The chart below shows the age that our beliefs are formed and who influences us at various ages of our development.

Ages	Individuals who influences you
0–7	parents and caregivers
8–13	teachers, heroes, athletes, actors, musicians
14–20	peers

After age twenty-one, beliefs are already established, but individuals may begin to test their old beliefs and change them.

The picture below, which shows an iceberg, gives you a visual illustration of how your beliefs are formed and acted upon. The picture clearly shows that our beliefs are below the surface, yet we know they are responsible for playing a significant role in controlling our lives. The tip of the iceberg (the portion visible above the water) represents our behaviors; the portion above the black line represents our thinking pattern. However, the portion below the surface (under the black line) represents our beliefs. As you can see, the largest portion of the iceberg is represented by our beliefs—the portion below the surface.

It is clear that our behavior is directly correlated with our core beliefs. By now, you may be starting to identify personal experiences that have caused many of your distorted beliefs. Take some time to reflect on your early childhood experiences.

List any distorted beliefs that were formed due to your personal experience:

_____
_____
_____
_____
_____
_____
_____
_____
_____
_____
_____

Two

Is Toxic Shame Holding You Back?

All of us experience shame at various times in our lives. You may feel ashamed when you get caught in a lie, cheat on an exam, betray a friend's trust, or act inappropriately when you're angry. Feeling ashamed is a normal response to behavior that you deem to be wrong or foolish. This is a healthy form of shame that, if used properly, can help you learn from your mistakes and make better choices. However, there is another type of shame—toxic shame—that can interfere with your ability to progress and achieve your personal and professional goals. Toxic shame is the belief that you are a worthless, inferior, or inherently bad person.

The chart below highlights the differences between healthy shame and toxic shame. As indicated below, healthy shame allows us to know our limits, discover our areas of growth, and reflect on our poor behavior for the purposes of change. Toxic shame, on the other hand, limits our ability to make healthy changes and prevents us from achieving our personal or professional desires.

Healthy Shame	Toxic Shame
I made a bad choice. I'll do better next time.	I'm bad, and I can't change.
I made a mistake but it doesn't define me.	I'm a mistake.

I made my friend angry but I'm not an awful person.	I'm awful.
I failed the test but I'm not a failure.	I'm a failure.

Children who were exposed to traumas such as abuse, neglect, rejection, or abandonment are more susceptible to developing toxic shame. According to John Bradshaw in the DVD entitled *Shame and Addiction*, toxic shame only occurs when we are hurt by significant figures in our lives. When children experience their parents or caregivers as unsafe, unreliable, or neglectful, toxic shame is formed. This is because children oftentimes blame their caregiver's lack of caring, protection, and dependability on themselves. This leads these children to believe that they are worthless or inferior or, worse yet, that they deserve their abuse.

As you become an adult, these beliefs don't just go away. Like a bad recording, these beliefs continue to plague your subconscious thinking and run your life. In order to free yourself from these erroneous beliefs and move forward, you must replace your negative beliefs with positive thoughts about yourself. This can be done by speaking your daily affirmations and forming healthy, trusting, and loving relationships with others. These relationships, in turn, will provide you with a corrective experience that will help heal and rewrite the negative messages from your past.

Toxic shame is usually passed down from significant others (such as mothers, fathers, or care providers) in your life. Listed below are some ways that shaming is passed down to others. Check off all that apply to your upbringing.

___ neglect
___ harsh criticism
___ blame
___ humiliation (especially in front of others)
___ teasing or tormenting
___ use of the silent treatment

___ disgusted looks
___ rejection
___ isolation

Did you experience any of these shaming messages growing up? How did the experience affect you? (How did you feel? Did it change your behavior?)

_____
_____
_____
_____
_____
_____
_____
_____
_____
_____

In order to change your self-defeating beliefs into healthy beliefs, you have to become aware of your internal dialogue, or self-talk. You can't control what others say about you, but you can control what you say to and about yourself. Be intentional about your thoughts and language. Only say positive things about yourself. Change will not happen overnight, but as you modify your self-talk, you will begin to notice that your negative messages begin to turn into healthy ones.

Healthy Relationships Are Vital to Your Recovery

What are healthy relationships? If you grew up in a dysfunctional home or environment, it is perfectly reasonable to assume that you may not know how to assess the relationships in your life. Below is a list of elements of a healthy relationship. Use it to evaluate your past and current relationships.

Healthy Relationships

- Both people get equal benefits out of the relationship. Neither person feels like he or she is being used or taken advantage of.
- You are treated with respect and kindness.
- You are accepted fully for who you are. You feel free to be your true self, flaws and all.
- The other person is not possessive of you or your time.
- The other person encourages you to pursue other friendships and interests.
- The other person motivates you to keep moving forward when you are struggling or feeling down.
- The other person encourages you to set goals and celebrates your successes.
- The other person is not competitive with you or jealous of you.
- The other person acknowledges when he or she is wrong and apologizes.
- The other person allows you to express your feelings—good or bad—without fear of rejection or retaliation.
- The other person forgives you freely and doesn't hold your mistakes against you.
- You trust the other person and feel safe (physically and emotionally) with him or her.

In the next exercise, you will list all the healthy people whom you currently have in your life. Use the list above to decide if they are healthy. The key here is that these individuals must be supportive of you. They shouldn't be judgmental, shaming, or critical people. If you don't have any healthy people, don't panic. You can create realistic action steps to meet new people. We recommend that you take a leap of faith and attend church, local meet-up groups, volunteer activities, 12-step support groups, or community-college classes to meet new people.

If you need to add members to your support group, you can move on to the exercise on page 14, Assessing Your Readiness for Change, while you're building your supports. Don't forget to come back to this section once you are ready. Establishing healthy relationships is a vital component to your long-term success.

List the people who will support you.

1.
2.
3.
4.
5.

Look over your list, and select an individual to become your mentor. Your mentor will be responsible for holding you accountable for old behaviors and helping you get through the exercises in this workbook. Your mentor should be an individual you feel comfortable sharing your secrets (fears and traumas) with.

The others on your list will become a part of your support group. They will help you become comfortable getting to know yourself and doing fun things. They are healthy friends. In the next week, make sure that you set up some time to meet with these individuals and ask them to support you in your recovery process. This may be challenging if you aren't used to asking others for help or support. However, if you truly want to be freed from your past baggage, you will need to take this healthy risk and reach out to your friends and family.

Name of person	Time of meeting	Location of meeting

As long as you isolate yourself, you will be unable to break the chains of toxic shame that hold you in bondage. You must come to understand that the key to your healing is your ability to form healthy and trusting relationships. The more supportive relationships you engage in, the healthier you will become. Through these relationships, you will begin to believe that you deserve happiness and fulfillment in your life. And, just as importantly, you will come to accept the truth about your situation—you were a victim, and you didn't deserve what happened to you.

Helpful Suggestions for Overcoming Toxic Shame

- Practice self-acceptance. Begin to accept yourself just the way you are as you work on areas you may want to change (such as losing weight, eliminating negative self-talk, and so on). Remember that you deserve the good things in life.
- Be patient with and kind to yourself. This is a process, not an event, and it will take time. Develop a healthy relationship with your higher power, and affirm yourself using the Word of God.
- Use only positive talk to yourself about yourself.
- Praise yourself for your accomplishments. You don't have to wait for others to tell you that you did a good job.
- Get positive support from others. Find healthy individuals who will encourage and support you and do fun activities with you. Consider attending a 12-step group for additional support. Don't hang out with individuals who are not supportive.
- Take responsibility for your mistakes, and be kind to yourself. Acknowledge your mistakes, accept the consequences, learn from them, and keep moving forward. Everyone makes mistakes.

- Take care of yourself by eating healthy, and nurture yourself by practicing self-care. Be aware of your physical appearance, and exercise. When you feel good about yourself, you create a positive attitude. Take pride in how you look and the way carry yourself.
- Set healthy boundaries for yourself. Associate with individuals who are positive and encouraging—individuals you can share your life experience with and feel comfortable socializing with. (Note: boundary setting will be discussed in more detail in chapter 3, "Understanding Codependency.")
- Start this journey today!

In this next exercise, we would like for you to assess your readiness for change. In order for sustainable change to occur, you must acknowledge your problem areas and commit to doing something about them. Be as honest as possible in answering the following questions:

1. What have you learned so far?
2. Do you believe that you can truly change? Why or why not?
3. How committed are you to this process?
4. What is your greatest fear or barrier associated with completing this workbook?
5. How will your life improve if you change your beliefs?

Assessing My Readiness for Change

_____
_____
_____
_____
_____
_____

The Complete Tool Kit For Personal and Professional Success

Your answers to these questions will determine your next steps in this workbook. For instance, if you don't truly believe that you can change, you have two choices. You can continue to work on yourself, despite your lack of belief in the process, or you can quit now and remain the same. The choice is yours. We sincerely hope that you will decide to stick with us and allow us to help you work through your fear or ambivalence.

If you decide to stop, we wish you well. We welcome you to pick up this workbook again when you are ready.

Three

DEVELOPING HEALTHY SELF-ESTEEM

You have to believe in yourself.

As you continue on this journey to wholeness, you will begin to discover some self-defeating beliefs surrounding your self-esteem. These beliefs may be preventing you from achieving your personal or professional goals. As we discuss self-esteem, you will uncover how your beliefs are affecting your self-image today.

Several years ago, I had the privilege of working with a client who had graduated from a prestigious college and had a successful career. Despite her outward success, however, she had very low self-esteem. Her identity was wrapped up in her career, and she had no healthy relationships at work or outside of work.

This woman grew up in a very dysfunctional family. As a child, she was told by her father on a regular basis that she was worthless, unlovable, and stupid. These self-defeating messages became her reality as a child. She internalized these negative messages and accepted them as truth. As a result, her self-esteem was solely based on her performance and others' opinions of her. These self-defeating beliefs continued to run her life as an adult, and she became stuck in a self-defeating cycle. She became a workaholic to prevent herself from focusing on her lack of a healthy social life or close family relationships. Her whole life revolved around her job.

Does this story sound familiar? If so, you must remember that if you can't love yourself unconditionally, you won't allow others to love you that way. You will keep others at arm's length or push them away altogether. This is what most individuals with low self-esteem do.

Is Your Self-Esteem Positive or Negative?

If you have positive or high self-esteem, you view yourself as a worthwhile individual. You realize that your worth is not based on your performance, career, education, income, good looks, or money, but on who you are.

If you have negative or low self-esteem, you view yourself as a worthless individual whose value is based on personal accomplishments.

Is your self-esteem positive or negative? Why? Write your thoughts in the space below.

_____
_____
_____
_____
_____
_____
_____
_____
_____
_____
_____
_____
_____

Negative self-esteem can manifest as an inferiority complex and can cause some of the following unhealthy behaviors. Check all that apply to you.

_____ sensitive to others' opinions
_____ likely to blame others for personal mistakes or shortcomings

____ self-critical and critical of others
____ unable to accept compliments
____ isolated, shy, and fearful
____ afraid of rejection
____ likely to compare self to others
____ dominated by negative self-talk

Did you check any of the behaviors listed above? If yes, describe how they are affecting your self-esteem today:
_____
_____
_____
_____
_____
_____
_____
_____

Your self-esteem is driven by your self-perceptions in other areas.

We are going to discuss four self-perceptions that may be affecting your self-esteem in a negative way. Check the ones you need to work on.

1. ____ **Identity**. A strong sense of self allows you to know "who you are," what you like and don't like, and what's important to you.
2. ____ **Self-Acceptance**. Self-acceptance involves embracing both your strengths and your weakness. If you accept yourself fully, you focus on your strengths and work to improve your weaknesses. You don't beat yourself up for everything you do wrong, and you learn from your mistakes.
3. ____ **Attitude and Behavior**. It is important to act in accordance with your core beliefs—to remain authentic to yourself and not act or

behave in ways you think others want you to in order to fit in. Your actions are a reflection of your personal desires.

4. ____ **Personal Values.** People with integrity use their personal values to guide their interactions with others. They do what they feel is right in every situation. Do your values motivate you to honor and respect others as well as be fair and honest in your business dealings?

What self-perception do you need to work on?
_____
_____
_____
_____
_____
_____
_____

List some practical things you can do to grow in those areas.
_____
_____
_____
_____
_____
_____
_____
_____
_____

People with positive self-esteem behave in the following ways. Check all that apply to you.

____ I take responsibility for my own feeling and actions.
____ I accept compliments graciously and say "thank you."

_____ I listen to feedback without becoming angry. (I don't have to agree with the comments.)
_____ I make decisions based on my own values and beliefs (even if others don't agree).
_____ I take good care of myself both physically and emotionally.
_____ I give honest praise and compliments to encourage others.
_____ I am willing to take healthy risks that challenge me to grow.
_____ I accept my mistakes and the consequences.
_____ I have a sense of humor that doesn't hurt others.
_____ I listen with the intent of understanding what others are saying.
_____ I don't dwell on past failures.

What are you most proud of about yourself? List your positive characteristics below:

_____
_____
_____
_____
_____
_____
_____
_____
_____
_____
_____
_____

If you are struggling with your self-esteem, listed below are some strategies that maybe helpful to you.

1. **Stop being self-critical**. When you put yourself down, you reinforce negative beliefs about yourself. When you affirm yourself, you begin to create a healthy self-image.

The Complete Tool Kit For Personal and Professional Success

2. **Be patient and gentle with yourself.** Being patient with yourself is essential as you learn new ways of thinking. Treat yourself as you would someone you really care about. You're worth it.
3. **Keep your thoughts positive.** Gently change your negative thoughts about yourself to positive thoughts. Living with negative self-talk leads to unhappiness and depression.
4. **Praise yourself.** Praise yourself whenever possible. Keep a daily journal that tracks your daily accomplishments. Even small accomplishments—waking up on time, having a pleasant conversation with a coworker, going for a walk—are important to write down.
5. **Be supportive of yourself.** Find ways to support yourself, such as practicing self-care and reaching out to healthy friends. It takes strength to ask for help when you need it.
6. **Be kind to yourself when you make mistakes.** When you make a mistake, admit that you made it, and accept the consequences. Don't beat yourself up over it. Let it go, and learn from it. After all, everyone makes mistakes.
7. **Take care of yourself.** Eat healthy and exercise regularly. Exercise helps improve your mood and helps you feel better about yourself. Remember, your body is the temple of God.
8. **Forgive yourself.** Forgive yourself for your past mistakes, and forgive everyone who has hurt you. Affirm yourself by saying the following: "I love you. I really love [your name], and I am going to take care of you."
9. **Do fun activities.** Try new things, and find new ways to have fun, such as hiking, bowling, swimming, and so on.
10. **Start the process today**. Don't wait until tomorrow to work on your goals. If you wait until you "feel like" doing something, it will never get done. You deserve to be the best person you can be right now, so don't put it off. Don't wait! Start today.

This process won't happen overnight; it will require patience and perseverance. But if you stay encouraged, are kind to yourself, and remain consistent, you will succeed. Remember, this is a journey and not a one-time event.

Four

UNDERSTANDING CODEPENDENCY

The next area that we will examine is codependency. Codependency is a learned behavior that develops when someone lives alongside another codependent individual—a drug addict, an alcoholic, a gambler, a disabled individual—or is raised in a dysfunctional environment. It affects individuals' ability to have healthy relationships with themselves and others.

Individuals suffering from codependency don't have healthy boundaries, and their greatest desire is to be accepted and loved by others. They will go to any length to get love and acceptance. According to *Rapha's 12-Step Program for Overcoming Codependency*, codependents grow up with three unspoken rules in the home: (1) don't talk, (2) don't feel, and (3) don't trust anyone.

If you are codependent, the people you gravitate to are usually codependent individuals as well. Codependents are highly insecure and have a difficult time interacting with healthy individuals. Their fear of rejection is so strong that they wear a mask of normalcy to make others think they are okay.

Codependency is an area that I personally struggled with when I was younger. When I was nine, my father had a stroke, and it caused my family dynamics to change. I had to grow up faster than my older siblings because my mother needed help with the younger children. It was at this point that my codependency started. I became a big enabler, a codependent who gravitates toward other codependent individuals in order to "rescue" and "fix" them.

Codependents can be one of two types. First is the enabler, a codependent person who attempts to rescue other people or fix their problems even though they are capable of solving their own problems. Enablers need to feel needed in their relationships and don't feel comfortable in equal relationships.

Second is the needy person. Some codependent people want others to take care of them and do everything for them.

Codependents have a hard time believing that they can be loved, so they settle for being needed.

Below are some examples of codependency.

Sue's husband left her with two children and no money. Sue didn't have a job; however, she did have supportive family members in another city. Despite having supportive family, Sue didn't want to ask her family for help because she didn't want to move out of the area. Consequently, Sue asked her friend Mary to lease a house for her and her two children.

Mary had concerns about leasing the house for her unemployed friend, but she did it anyway. Mary lied on the leasing paperwork and put the lease in her name, along with all the utility bills. During this process, Mary was thinking to herself, "How is Sue going to pay the rent without a job?" Even though Mary's better judgment warned her to avoid this situation, she honored Sue's request because of her need to feel needed. The desire to feel needed overshadowed Mary's own common sense and pushed her to sign the paperwork. Not surprisingly, this situation didn't end well for Mary. Sue failed to pay the rent and the utilities. Just as Mary had suspected, the mounting bills fell on Mary and her family to pay. Mary was eventually able to get Sue to move out of the house, but not before she incurred thousands of dollars in expenses and damages.

This is a prime example of how codependents put others' needs before their own and those of their families. Mary's actions not only affected her; they negatively affected her family's financial stability as well. Again, the codependent's mission is to be accepted by others, and these individuals will do almost anything for acceptance and love.

John works a twelve-hour shift and doesn't typically get home until eight. His daughter Carol, a junior in high school, waits until he gets home to tell him that she needs him to complete her take-home math final. John later learns that Carol went to the movies with her friends after school. Not wanting to confront Carol or make her angry, John completes his daughter's exam for her. Although John is very upset about his daughter's behavior, he doesn't want to risk upsetting Carol or causing her to feel bad about herself, so he chooses not to share his feelings with her. Instead he pretends that everything is okay and continues to bail his daughter out of difficult situations.

In this scenario John is the enabler, and Carol is the needy codependent.

Below is a list of codependent characteristics. Check all that apply to you.

_____ I say yes to things that I want to say no to.
_____ I enable others' negative behaviors.
_____ I do things for others that they can do for themselves.
_____ I meet others' needs before my own.
_____ I have low self-esteem.
_____ I am controlling, and yet I am controlled by others.
_____ I blame others for my problems.
_____ I manipulate others to get what I want.
_____ I distrust everyone.
_____ I need everything to be perfect.
_____ I have intimacy problems.
_____ I suffer from stress-related physical illnesses.
_____ I am indecisive.
_____ I have a hard time asking for help.

What did you find out about yourself? Were you surprised by any of your answers?

_____
_____
_____
_____

The Complete Tool Kit For Personal and Professional Success

_____
_____
_____
_____
_____
_____

Make sure that you are consistently affirming yourself daily. It is very easy to get off track and start refocusing on your current struggles. Don't allow this to happen. Remain committed to changing your beliefs and improving your life. If you keep moving forward, you will reach your desired destination.

Listed below are some common codependent beliefs and consequences that Pat Springle discusses in *Rapha's 12-Step Program for Overcoming Codependency*.

False Beliefs	Consequences of False Beliefs
I must meet certain standards in order to feel good about myself.	fear of failure, perfectionism, overemphasis on drive to succeed, manipulation of others to achieve success, withdrawal from healthy risks
I must have the approval of certain others to feel good about myself.	fear of rejection, attempts to please others at any cost, oversensitivity to criticism, withdrawal from others to avoid punishment
Those who fail (including me) are unworthy of love and deserve to be punished.	fear of punishment and propensity to punish others, blame of self and others for personal failure, withdrawal from God and fellow believers, overemphasis on avoiding punishment
I am what I am. I cannot change. I am hopeless.	shame, hopelessness, apathy, feelings of inferiority, passivity, loss of creativity, isolation, and withdrawal from others

Review the distorted beliefs and consequences listed above. Can you identify any that apply to you? If you can, write new beliefs and consequences that you can work on. An example is provided below:

New Belief: I can do all things I put my mind to.
New Consequences: I have increased confidence and the desire to follow through.

Note: to change the outcome, you must identify the belief and change the belief.

New Beliefs
_____
_____
_____
_____
_____

New Consequences
_____
_____
_____
_____
_____

The Importance of Setting Healthy Boundaries

Individuals who grew up in dysfunctional families usually don't have healthy boundaries. The lack of consistent structure prevented them from understanding what healthy boundaries are.

A boundary can be defined as an emotional line that others are not allowed to cross, the emotional and physical space you need in order to feel safe, or a physical distance you maintain between you and others that makes you feel comfortable.

Below is a chart of unhealthy and healthy boundaries. Review them, and identify any unhealthy boundaries that you may need to address.

Unhealthy Boundaries	Healthy Boundaries
I can't say no, even when I don't want to do something.	I have the right to say no to things I don't want to do.
If I don't do everything in my relationship, it will fall apart.	It is the responsibility of each person in the relationship to do his or her fair share to keep the relationship healthy.
I will never trust anyone again.	I am willing to be open and trust others and try to foster a new, healthy relationship even if I was hurt in the past. I can use effective communication to express myself and set healthy boundaries.
I feel guilty when I do activities on my own and leave my friends or family out.	I have the right to explore my own interests or hobbies with others and by myself.

How to Establish Healthy Boundaries

Here are some suggestion on establishing healthy boundaries between yourself and others.

- Identify which boundaries you are violating or ignoring. If you have never had boundaries, ask yourself this question: "Does this behavior make me feel uncomfortable or uneasy?" If the answer is yes, your boundaries are being crossed.
- Identify the distorted thinking and beliefs that allow you to tolerate this behavior. Ask yourself, "Why do I allow this person to treat me this way?" This will help you identify the distorted belief. One of the main reasons many people don't set boundaries is fear of rejection.
- Identify new, healthy beliefs that will encourage you to change your problematic behaviors. This will allow you to maintain healthy boundaries. Also remember that boundaries teach others how to treat you. They will be able understand what you will or won't tolerate in the relationships, and this will allow you to develop healthy relationships. You deserve to be treated with respect.

List the boundaries that you need to address and develop a plan to set those boundaries?

_____
_____
_____
_____
_____
_____
_____
_____
_____
_____

When you are ready, assertive communication is a healthy way to establish clear boundaries.

The goal of an assertive communicator is to share feelings and desires in a nonthreatening way—to honestly but respectfully express your needs or wants to the other person. Don't try to set a boundary when you are angry. When setting boundaries, you should remain calm and be respectful.

Below are examples of assertive messages for setting boundaries:

- "I don't like when you talk down to me." This statement stays focused on the undesirable behavior (talking down) and doesn't attack the person.
- "I feel hurt." This statement uses "I" instead of "you." Such statements allow you to take responsibility for you own feelings.
- "I will not tolerate such behavior because it is disrespectful." This statement describes how the behavior is negatively affecting you.
- "I want you to talk to me respectfully." Effective messages share your needs, wants, desires, or wishes with the other person.
- "If you can't talk to me respectfully, I won't hang out with you anymore." Statements such as this indicate a clear boundary that will be put in place if the request is not honored.

Please do not set a boundary that you are unwilling to carry out. Remember that threats don't work. The use of threats will undermine your efforts and lead the other person to feel manipulated or controlled by your actions. Additionally, refrain from setting boundaries when you are angry or emotional. This will lead to better outcomes. By staying calm, respectful, and direct, you are ensuring that the other person has the best opportunity to hear the message you need to get across. We encourage you get someone from your support group to hold you accountable for keeping new boundaries.

How Do You Break the Cycle of Codependency?

1. Once you become aware of your codependent beliefs and behaviors, you can begin to slowly change them. Keep your self-talk positive, and continue affirming yourself. These are the first steps in this process.
2. Become willing to accept yourself and eventually love yourself by affirming yourself and surrounding yourself with supportive individuals. You may want to attend a college class, join a 12-step support group, attend church, or join a community group to meet new people to try something new. When you first start out, this will be uncomfortable, and this is normal. However, taking healthy risk is very healthy.
3. Be responsible for your choices, both good and bad. Don't beat yourself up for the bad choices. Learn from them, and keep moving forward. Everyone makes mistakes.
4. Take time to do nice things for yourself. Learn to have fun and enjoy life. Try new things such as hiking, gardening, bowling, painting, or other activities that may be fun for you. Remember, taking the first step is the hardest part of the process. Once you take the risk to go to your first event, it gets easier every time.
5. Develop healthy boundaries. Boundaries teach others how to treat you, and they will keep you safe.

Five

Managing Your Anger

Many people try to avoid their anger because they don't realize that anger is a normal and healthy emotion. Anger *is* normal. It is defined as a feeling of displeasure or hostility. In essence, anger is simply a warning bell that lets you know when something is wrong. In this regard, anger is neither right nor wrong. However, how you respond when you are angry will determine whether your behavior is right or wrong.

In most cases, anger is a secondary emotion. The first response to a negative situation may actually be hurt, disappointment, shame, embarrassment, rejection, or jealousy. When one of those emotions occurs, many individuals react in anger. Therefore, people look upon anger as something bad. Everyone gets angry, but if we don't react in an aggressive manner (lashing out, screaming, or throwing things), we think we don't have anger issues. In this chapter, we will discuss different ways anger can be expressed and how it can affect you and others.

Write your definition of *anger* in the space below. What makes you angry?
_____
_____
_____
_____

The Complete Tool Kit For Personal and Professional Success

Do you express your anger in an unhealthy manner? If the answer to that question is yes, what has your anger cost you (e.g., friendships, jobs, and so on)?

Anger involves three elements. Let's discuss each one in more detail.

> **Your emotions.** Anger is a secondary emotion. We usually feel other emotions first—hurt, shame, disappointment, rejection, frustration, or embarrassment—before we become angry. Taking some time to calm down and process your feelings will help you find out what you are really feeling. Unfortunately, most people do not process their anger; therefore, they do not get in touch with their real feelings or understand why they are angry.
>
> **Your thinking.** You can cause your anger to intensify or lessen, depending on what you are thinking. No one makes you angry; you push your own buttons. You may wonder how this is possible. The fact is that the things you say to yourself cause you to get angry. This

self-talk, which comes from your beliefs, causes you to respond appropriately, passively, aggressively, or passive-aggressively.

Your body. Anger causes physical symptoms in your body, such as increased heart rate, muscle tension, and increased blood pressure. Do you know what the physical signs are in your body when you get angry?

Knowing how your body responds when you're angry is essential in learning how to manage anger appropriately. When you feel your body reacting to a perceived threat, you should take a time-out to calm down (if possible). Becoming aware of the physical signs of anger in your body gives you an opportunity to think before responding in an unhealthy manner.

Your beliefs drive your emotions and can cause you to react in a variety of ways. For example, if you grew up in an environment where it wasn't okay to get angry, as an adult you may suppress your feelings and avoid your anger. However, if you change your beliefs about your anger, your behavior will follow. Remember, no one but you can make you angry.

How was anger handled in your home as you were growing up? How do you handle anger today? What are some beliefs about anger you need to change?

_____
_____
_____
_____
_____
_____
_____
_____
_____
_____
_____
_____
_____
_____

There is evidence that anger can be harmful to your health. According to WebMD, the symptoms described below are associated with unresolved anger:

- headaches
- sleep difficulties
- high blood pressure
- digestive problems
- tense muscles
- inability to concentrate
- weight changes (gain or loss)

If you are experiencing any of these symptoms, ask yourself if you are harboring anger toward a situation, God, another person, or even yourself.

Unforgiveness is oftentimes a form of unresolved anger, one that weakens you physically, mentally, and emotionally. It is literally like drinking poison and expecting someone else to die from it. Although you may hope or even believe that the target of your anger is suffering, the truth is that you are hurting yourself far more. Medical researchers now believe that the stress and hostility related to unresolved anger can lead to heart attacks. Therefore, it is very important to learn to manage your anger in a healthy way. At the end of this session, we will discuss some healthy ways to manage your anger.

List any health issues below that you are struggling with. Do you believe that unforgiveness may be the root cause of these ailments? Why or why not?

_____
_____
_____
_____
_____
_____
_____
_____
_____

If unforgiveness is a problem in your life, the section in the workbook on forgiveness will address it in more detail.

Different Anger Responses

SUPPRESSION

The suppressive anger response is a conscious act that allows individuals to pretend they're not angry. They stuff their anger, and this can become toxic to them and others. Those who practice this style internalize their anger because they believe that it isn't okay to get angry. They pretend they aren't angry to avoid conflicts that can lead to an argument.

Over time, their anger will eventually erupt and hurt both them and others. People with this anger response can develop physical conditions such as ulcers, high blood pressure, and heart problems. Emotionally, they are usually depressed and very unhappy.

EXPRESSION

The expressive anger response involves acting out, yelling, screaming, throwing, or breaking things in order to intimidate others. For example, a father may come home from work angry at his boss and scream at his two-year-old son for spilling milk on the floor. He takes his aggression out on the child rather than talking directly to his boss about his frustrations.

People with this type of anger response are usually on edge and uptight. They can be volatile and unpredictable. These individuals can become physically abusive to children, spouses, and others. A friendship with such an individual is very intense. These individuals don't take personal responsibility for their behavior and instead blame others. Their friendships are filled with hostility that explodes with the slightest provocation and in many cases negatively affects the wrong person. In many homes where there is violence, children learn these ways of handling their anger, and these behaviors continue into adulthood. This anger may be harmful to others and or destructive to property.

Repression

The repressive anger response is rooted in simple denial. Individuals who repress their anger often times don't acknowledge they are angry and often substitute their anger with alcohol, drugs, food, sex, or work. They have a very difficult time expressing their anger directly, and they usually become masters at avoiding theirs' or others' anger. They use unhealthy alternatives to cope with their anger and oftentimes become addicted to their anger substitutes.

Confession

Finally we come to a healthy response to anger—confession. Some individuals take responsibility for their feelings and are able to express them in a healthy way. They express themselves assertively—not aggressively. Being assertive allows them to state their concerns and needs clearly. These individuals have the confidence to express themselves without feeling the need to physically or emotionally hurt the other person's feelings or try to control the situation.

Here are the four parts of an assertive message.

1. Describe the behavior: *When you talk about me negatively to your friends...*
2. Use "I" statements to express your feelings: *I feel angry...*
3. Describe how the behavior affects you: *because it's hurtful to me and I feel disrespected by you.*
4. State your desires, wants, or needs: *I want you to stop doing that.*

How do you handle anger?

___
___
___
___
___
___
___

Is your response healthy for you?

_____
_____
_____
_____
_____
_____
_____

Are you willing to change? What are you willing to do?

_____
_____
_____
_____
_____
_____
_____

Use your support group to help you identify your anger responses. Do you need to change your behavior? Listed below are some tips for managing anger. Write your plans here.

_____
_____
_____
_____
_____
_____

Tips for Anger Management

1. Take a time-out and count to ten backward before responding when you are angry. Counting backward forces you to focus on the numbers and takes your mind off what made you angry.

2. Once you're calm, go back and express yourself assertively. It's healthy to express your frustration in a none confrontational way.
3. Go for a walk, swim, or go to the gym. Physical activities are a great outlet for dealing with anger. They reduce the stress that is caused by anger.
4. Listen with the intent of understanding what the other person is saying. Don't personalize; you don't have to agree with what is being said.
5. If you are very angry, think carefully before you say anything. Otherwise you may say something that you'll regret later. It may also be helpful to write down what you want to say so that you can stick to the issue and be assertive. When you're angry, it is very easy to get sidetracked.
6. Don't hold grudges. Forgiving the other person will help both of you. It's unrealistic to expect people to behave exactly as you want them to. We all respond differently based on our beliefs.
7. Use "I" statements when describing the problem. This will help you avoid criticizing or blaming others.
8. Relaxation techniques are very helpful in reducing stress and calming you down. Practice deep-breathing exercises.
9. Listen to soothing or calming music.

The Power of Forgiveness

Forgiveness is a major issue for many people. Yet forgiveness is necessary for the healing process to begin. It is very important for you to acknowledge and accept the fact that you were deeply hurt by family members, peers, friends, or others. You must also be willing to make a personal choice to let the pain from the hurtful event go.

Letting go of resentment doesn't make you weak, nor does it mean that you are okay with what happened to you. Rather, it means that you give up the right to hold resentments and plot revenge against those who hurt you.

Sometimes the person you have to forgive is dead. One of the exercises I encourage is to write a letter to the dead person. The letter should tell the person how his or her behavior affected you. You should include everything you want the person to know and end the letter by telling the person whom you have chosen to forgive him or her in order to move forward in your own life. You can burn the letter or put it in a balloon and release it. Hopefully this will help to bring you closure.

Real healing begins when you become willing to speak openly about your pain and acknowledge your feelings surrounding your past hurts, anger, rage, hate, or sadness. This may bring to the surface a lot of old pain and sadness, but, if you allow it, an internal healing process will begin to take place. Make sure you use your support group if needed.

Taking ownership of those painful feelings will allow you to get in touch with the painful events from your past and begin to process them.

List the individuals who hurt you and describe how it impacted your life.

_____
_____
_____
_____
_____
_____
_____
_____
_____

Forgiveness is an internal process, and it is the ultimate act of self-love. It isn't about the individuals who hurt you but about how you will handle the pain associated with your hurt. Holding on to resentments keeps you stuck and prevents you from truly moving forward in your life. You must realize that unforgiveness will produce in you the very thing that you hate in the other person. Take, for example. children who were abused by their parents. They likely grew up hating their parents and swore they would never be like them. Yet when these children themselves become parents, many of them exhibit the same character defects their parents possessed.

Forgiving someone doesn't mean that you need to continue to interact with him or her. In fact, it may be in your best interest to let go of the relationship if you deem it to be unhealthy and beyond repair. Unfortunately, some individuals aren't emotionally or physically safe to be around, and they shouldn't be an active presence in your life. This is precisely why establishing healthy boundaries is key in your healing process. It allows you to take care of yourself and eliminate toxic individuals from your life.

Now choose to release the individuals who hurt you and let them go. Write a letter of forgiveness for each of them. Remember, forgiveness doesn't make you weak.

_____
_____
_____
_____
_____
_____
_____
_____
_____
_____
_____
_____
_____
_____
_____
_____

Six

Taking Accountability

If you truly want to prosper in all areas of your life, you must let go of the things that have held you in bondage and take accountability for the part you have played in your life's getting off track. The next phase of this journey calls for self-love, forgiveness, and maturity.

What is maturity? Maturity is making a judgment based on the ability to see the big picture. It means you are willing to pass up on the "fun for now" and choose to do the hard work required to accomplish your desired goal. Completing this workbook can be considered being mature on your part today. You are willing to face unpleasantness, frustration, discomfort, and defeat without giving up, and you continue to be responsible and dependable to ensure the task is completed because you have integrity.

If you are going to achieve your personal or professional goals, you must realize that you will have struggles along the way. However, these hardships will produce tremendous character within you if you allow them to.

Immature Behaviors

Listed below are some immature behaviors. Check all that apply to you.

The Complete Tool Kit For Personal and Professional Success

_____ I don't follow through on commitments, and I give up easily.
_____ I am unreliable and undependable.
_____ I break promises and use alibis as excuses for my behavior.
_____ I am disorganized.
_____ I waste time exploring possibilities because I am unwilling to do the work needed to achieve my goals.
_____ I won't take healthy risks needed to achieve goals.
_____ I want instant gratification. I don't want to work for what I want.
_____ I am loyal only when it benefits me.
_____ I am selfish and self-centered.
_____ I am manipulative.

Based on the number of items that you checked, what did you learn about yourself?

_____
_____
_____
_____
_____
_____
_____
_____
_____
_____
_____
_____
_____
_____
_____

Mature Behaviors

Listed below are some mature behaviors. Check all that apply to you.

_____ I am willing to confront my problems without attacking others.
_____ I live up to my commitments.

_____ I seek to find solutions to my problems.
_____ I express my feelings appropriately.
_____ I listen to others' feedback without personalizing.
_____ I take responsibility for my mistakes and learn from them.
_____ I give of myself in an effort to enhance my quality of life and that of my loved ones.
_____ I work well with others.
_____ I cooperate with others to achieve desired results.
_____ I allow others to give to me.

After reviewing the mature behaviors, what areas are you doing well in? It is very important for you to acknowledge the things you are doing well. Use your mature behaviors to affirm yourself also.

_____
_____
_____
_____
_____
_____

In order to fulfill your personal goals, you must be willing to acknowledge your character defects and break free of denial. This means that you need to get real with yourself about any addictions you may currently be struggling with.

What Is an Addiction?

Addiction is defined as the state of being enslaved to a habit, practice, or something that is psychologically or physically habit forming despite negative consequences.

Are you struggling with an addiction? There are many types of addictions. Check all that apply to you.

___ codependency (addiction to approval)
___ drugs
___ gambling
___ relationships (inability to feel complete without a relationship)
___ sex or pornography
___ fast money (thrill-seeking behavior)
___ shopping
___ food (emotional eating)
___ work (allowing work to define who you are)
___ exercise
___ criminal thinking

Are you struggling with any of the addictions listed above? How is addiction affecting you?

_____
_____
_____
_____
_____

You may ask what denial is. Denial is defined as a disbelief in the existence or reality in an individual's mind. It can be an unconscious defense mechanism used to reduce anxiety by denying feelings or facts that indicate a problem.

There are different types of denial; however, we will focus on four types that many immature individuals tend to use.

Simple denial. Many individuals are unaware of their own dishonesty. They don't realize they are lying. Lying for them is an unconscious way of avoiding pain.

Minimizing. Individuals who practice this kind of denial make problems appear to be less serious than they actually are.

Blaming. With this type of denial, the individual does not take responsibility for his or her actions. A problem is always someone else's fault.

Hostility. Hostile individuals use anger to get others to avoid uncomfortable topics and their negative attitude or behaviors.

Do you use any of these types of denial? What are you trying to hide when you use denial?

_____
_____
_____
_____
_____
_____
_____
_____

Manipulation

Another behavior that you need to be aware of is manipulation. Manipulation is the act of falsifying information to get what you want.

Lying and manipulating are compulsive behaviors associated with individuals who grew up in dysfunctional homes. Once you identify this dysfunctional trait, you need to work hard to eliminate it.

Manipulation is all about protecting, advancing, or feeding your self-centered desires. Individuals who use manipulation aren't concerned about anyone but themselves; it's all about getting their personal desires or needs met.

Manipulating others is one of the most destructive and hurtful behaviors that you can engage in. If you want to achieve your personal or professional goals, it is important to stop manipulating others.

Do you use manipulation to get what you want? Why?

Taking Responsibility for Your Choices

In order to gain the skills you need to be successful, you must take responsibility for your choices, both good and bad. Our perception of failure is misleading. Failure is making poor choices and not learning from the mistakes. Success, on the other hand, is not the absence of failure rather it is positively moving forward despite it.

It takes courage to change. Are you ready? What are some behaviors that you need to take responsibility for and change?

Seven

Pulling It All Together

The previous modules were selected to help you identify beliefs that were negatively affecting your personal or professional life. In many cases, you may have been totally unaware of those beliefs and their impact on your life. However, by becoming aware of them, you are more able to overcome those obstacles and achieve your goals.

Self-Nurturing

In order for you to maintain balance in your relationships, you must take care of yourself. You can't expect others to treat you well if you treat yourself poorly. Nurturing yourself will help you develop a healthy appreciation for your self-worth and abilities.

How much time do you spend doing pleasurable things alone? What are things that you enjoy doing for fun

_____
_____
_____

Empathetic Listening

If you are going to accomplish your life goals, you have to become an effective communicator. Communication is one of the key elements in a healthy relationship. Therefore, it is important that you know when it's appropriate to speak, listen, or sit and process information that is being shared.

Most people listen with the intent of replying. This isn't active listening, and it causes one to miss important information in the conversation.

Are you a good listener? Do you listen with the intent of replying or for understanding?

_____

_____

_____

_____

_____

To become an effective communicator, you must be aware of barriers to listening. Listed below are some common barriers to empathetic listening. Check off the ones that apply to you.

1. ____ I talk over other people or constantly interrupt them.
2. ____ I am focused on formulating my response rather than listening.
3. ____ I have a lot on my mind, so I am unable to stay focused.
4. ____ I am not emotionally available to listen.
5. ____ I jump to conclusions without all the facts.

Sometimes the speaker will put up barriers to listening. These include using a tone that comes across as sarcastic or disrespectful, making statements that seem threatening (such as "You better…" or "You must…"), or nagging—continuing to say the same thing over and over.

Make a list of things you plan to do to remove barriers that keep you from being an effective communicator.

_____
_____
_____
_____
_____
_____
_____
_____

You communicate in three different ways—verbal, written, and nonverbal. Nonverbal messages are conveyed through tone of voice, body language, facial expressions, use of interpersonal space, and gestures.

Listed below are the different communication styles and their basic coping strategies.

Communication Styles and Basis Coping Strategies

Passive

- avoids eye contact (looks down or away)
- gives in to others' requests
- puts others' needs first
- avoids conflict

Passive-Aggressive

- communicates indirectly
- stuffs feelings and eventually blows up
- seeks out to get revenge
- makes sarcastic remarks

Aggressive

- insensitive to others' needs or wants
- uses anger and hostility to intimidate others

Assertive

- uses eye contact
- communicates honestly and directly
- have healthy self-esteem
- uses "I" statements to express feelings
- respectful of others

What communication style do you use most of the time? Does this style allow you to get your information across in an effective manner?

_____
_____
_____
_____
_____
_____
_____
_____
_____

What Causes Conflict?

Many view conflict as harmful or hurtful, yet conflict is a normal part of life. Conflict can help others learn new things about you and allow you to set boundaries that help keep you safe.

The way we handle conflict is a learned behavior. It goes back to the environment we grew up in. Understanding why individuals respond the way they do can help us deal with conflict more effectively.

We will examine three causes of conflict to help you understand others' reactions to conflict better.

- **Assumptions**. It is unwise to jump to conclusions in relationships. Doing so leads to unnecessary confusion and hurt feelings. When you are uncertain about something, clarify it with the other person, and avoid making assumptions.
- **Different values and beliefs**. We all look at the world through our own lenses. If you grew up in a home where 10 percent of your income was saved and your partner grew up in a home where family members purchased whatever they wanted and saved nothing, this will cause conflict in the relationship. Different beliefs about money, child-rearing, and the like can cause conflict. Take time to get to understand others' values; this can help you understand their viewpoint.
- **Lack of knowledge.** Some people just don't know how to deal with conflict; therefore, in most cases they avoid conflict. You may be able to help such people develop the skills necessary to address and deal with conflict appropriately.

Really taking the time to understand people's values and beliefs can help you not react to situations in a negative way.

Assertive communication will help you become an effective communicator and help you handle conflict effectively. Effective communication is one of the keys to handling conflicts in a healthy way. Another key to handling conflict effectively is understanding the different conflict styles and determining how to best respond in each situation.

The Complete Tool Kit For Personal and Professional Success

There are five common styles of conflict resolution, and no style is right or wrong. Using the appropriate style to effectively handle problems is the key. Identify your conflict-resolution styles.

1. **Avoiding**. Avoiding a situation when you are angry can be helpful in many situations. It can prevent you from saying something that you will be sorry for. However, in some situations avoiding is not the best solution. It is not a good idea to avoid a situation that will not go away. Not dealing with a problem that continues to occur will become frustrating to you or others. In these situations, you should try one of the other conflicts styles to resolve the problem.
2. **Competitive**. Individuals who practice this style generally operate from a position of authority or power. This style is commonly used by parents, such as when they refuse to allow a child to do something that may hurt the child. It can also be seen in the workplace when a manager gives the team a directive to follow to complete a task and disregards his staff's input.
3. **Compromising**. In this conflict-resolution style, both parties give up something to find an acceptable solution for everyone.
4. **Collaborating**. This style acknowledges everyone's ideas and tries to meet the objective needs of everyone involved. This requires that everyone agrees with the end results, which means that this process can be very time-consuming.
5. **Accommodating**. Individuals who practice this style give up their own needs to meet the other person's needs. This style is okay when the outcome doesn't matter that much to you. However, if the outcome is important to you, you will eventually become resentful.

How do you handle conflict? What are some strategies you can use to handle conflict more effectively?

_____
_____

_____
_____
_____
_____
_____
_____
_____
_____
_____

Each conflict style can be useful in different situations. (For example, if I am very angry, I will try to avoid the other person until I calm down). You may have to work with healthy people in your support group to learn to deal with conflict in a healthy way. Don't be afraid to ask for help.

Below is an easy conflict-resolution strategy for intimate relationships. Most important is that you don't try to address the issue when you are angry. Your anger may be displayed in your tone, attitude, or body language. Make sure you are calm before you try to address the issue.

1. Use effective communication to state the problem or issue. Don't assume or use name-calling. Stay away from comments like "You always…" or "You never…" These can cause the other person to become defensive and stop listening. Remain calm.
2. Come up with several possible solutions to address the problem, and get buy-in from the other person.
3. Decide on a solution that you both agree with.
4. Implement the solution.
5. Follow up with the other person to ensure the solution is working for everyone.

Eight

WALKING IN VICTORY

Walking in victory means you are incorporating new skills into your personal and professional life. You are not allowing fear of disapproval or rejection to dominate your life and prevent you from standing up for your own opinions or beliefs. In the beginning, standing up for yourself may seem scary; however, with a strong support group, you can do it. This journey must include healthy people. You will need them to support and encourage you to help you continue moving forward.

Remember: this is a journey, not an event. Change will not happen overnight. It will take time, so be patient with you. You will not do everything perfectly, but with a strong support group and determination, you will be successful. Stay focused on your internal dialogue; keep your self-talk positive regardless of your emotions. Your self-talk will begin to create the new beliefs needed to transform your life.

My prayer is that you will begin to experience the freedom you were created to walk in. Keep walking toward your destiny. If you change your beliefs, your behavior will follow.

In summary, you should begin to display the following characteristics in your new relationships:

1. **Trustworthiness.** Others can trust that your yeses mean yes and your no means no.
2. **Responsibility.** You can be counted on to live up to your commitments and take responsibility for your choices, both good and bad.
3. **Honesty**. You tell the truth.
4. **Respect**. You treat others with dignity and respect even when you disagree with their ideas or comments.
5. **Intimacy**. You are open and transparent with your loved ones.
6. **Shared values**. You share your values and desires with others and gravitate to those who share similar values.
7. **Time Apart**. You take time out for yourself.

This workbook is a vehicle to get you started on your recovery journey. It will take time to get to your final destination. Therefore, it is very important that you utilize your support group and continue practicing the new skills you have learned. It is also important to remember that knowledge in and of itself isn't all that powerful—but applied knowledge is. It is up to you how you use the information you have been given. If you continue to apply the knowledge you have gained from this workbook, you will begin to achieve your personal and professional goals. May God bless you on your new journey.

Bibliography

American Psychological Association. "Controlling Anger Before It Controls You." Accessed December 8, 2016. http://www.apa.org/topics/anger/control.aspx?.

Burney, Roberts. "Setting personal boundaries." Accessed December 26, 2016. http://www.joy2meu.com/Personal _Boundaries.htm.

Bradshaw, John. *Addiction and Shame*. DVD. FMS Production. 2008.

Educational Reference. "What is self-esteem?" Accessed December 26, 2016. http://www. reference.com

Hermes, Sheila. *Art of Assertiveness*. DVD. Hazelden. 1998

Springle, Pat. *Rapha's 12-Step Program for Overcoming Codependency*. Texas: Rapha Publishing, 1990.

Thomas, K.W. & Kilman "5 Conflict Management Styles at a glance-source of light". Accessed 12/27/2016 http://www.sourceofinsight.com/conflict-management-styles.

Threewitt, Bruce. "Rebuilding Careers." Power Point 5/2010.

Made in the USA
Coppell, TX
15 December 2021